I Can Be Brave

Overcoming Fear, Finding Confidence, and Asserting Yourself

Written by
Holde Kreul

Illustrated by
Dagmar Geisler

Translated by
Andrea Jones Berasaluce

Sky Pony Press
New York

Visit our website at www.skyponypress.com.

10 9 8 7 6 5 4 3 2 1

Manufactured in China, February 2020
This product conforms to CPSIA 2008

Library of Congress Cataloging-in-Publication Data is available on file.

German Production Team: Officine Grafiche DeAgostini
Cover design by Andreas Henze and Daniel Brount
Cover illustration by Dagmar Geisler

Print ISBN: 978-1-5107-4661-9
Ebook ISBN: 978-1-5107-4672-5

Dear Adults!

"Look what I can do. Watch me!"

Children often shout this, and they are so proud of themselves when they do! Such moments are often viewed as minor by adults, but for children, they are usually a step forward. Having confidence in yourself means overcoming fear and being brave. This is—not only for children—difficult and often only possible with the support of an adult.

When a person has the courage to do something, it means they trust in their own abilities. A child, for example, feels: "This I can do, it's easier than I thought." Or: "I made a mistake. This I can't do alone, I need help."

Via the individual situations presented in this book, readers will be able to
see themselves. These situations are good conversation starters. While reading, children will become very conscious of themselves and will learn how to practice their social skills: for example, asserting themselves, drawing lines for themselves, learning to give in at times, and learning to approach others. Children who have confidence in themselves are less easily influenced by
others because their own personalities are stronger.

Holde Kreul

Do you want to hear about all the things we can do, and how we've found confidence in ourselves to do them?

For my birthday, I set the table almost all by myself. Mama was very surprised. Then when I helped clear it and wash the dishes, too, Mama's eyes grew wide.

I've jumped off a
three-foot-high diving board.
The first time,
I was pretty afraid.
Then I said to myself:
"Just do it!"
And it worked!

I don't pet Lumpi,
the Schröders' dog,
even though I'm allowed.
He always barks so loudly.
And I don't like that.

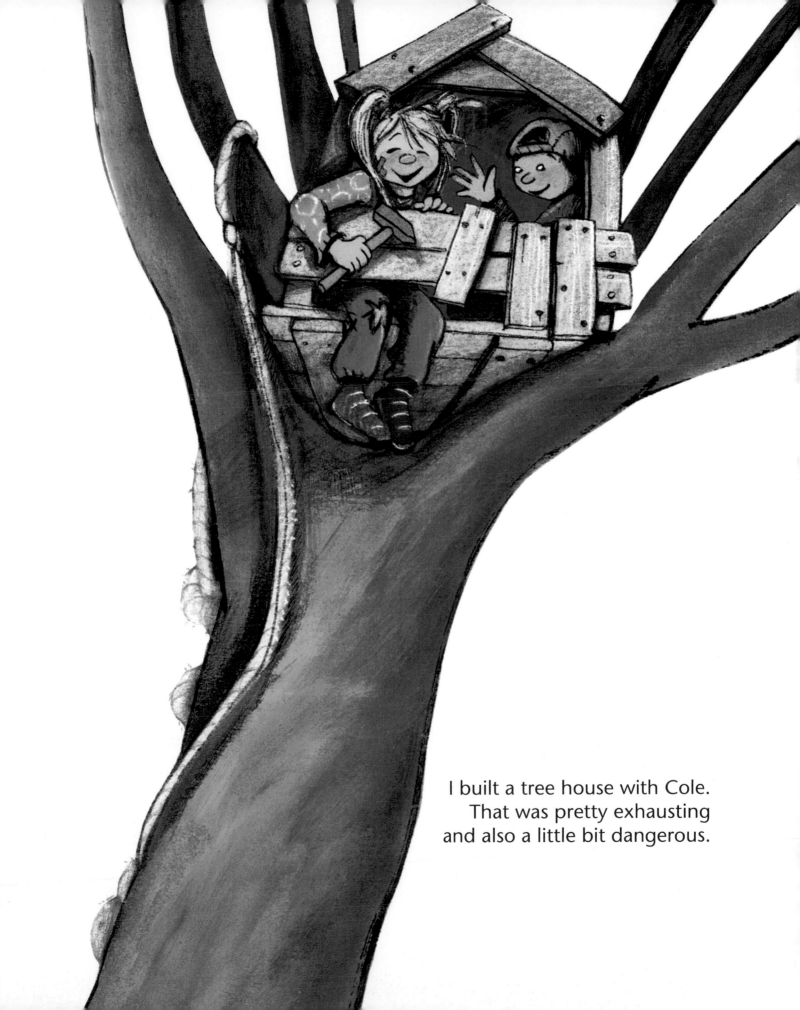

I built a tree house with Cole.
That was pretty exhausting
and also a little bit dangerous.

Mom + Dad
are with
Aunt Julia
555-0123

If I have the telephone number
and know where Mom and Dad are,
I can stay home alone. As long as I can call,
I have confidence in myself and
can stay home by myself.

We're happy and always very proud when we have achieved something.

Miriam is bigger than I am. She also knows much more
than I do and goes food shopping alone sometimes.
The first time I went shopping alone, I was totally excited.
After, I proudly told Miriam that it all went well.

At first, I couldn't skate well at all with roller blades. I kept falling down, over and over again. But then I practiced and practiced. Now I'm doing quite well.

I made myself a large, colorful kite. But it didn't fly.
Instead, it crashed down over and over again. I was so sad.

Andy's kite, however, flew right away.
It also had a much longer tail.

Andy then showed me how to fold the tail correctly.
And I paid close attention. Andy can make crafts better
than I can.

Andy wanted me to make a kite that was just like his.
But I really loved my colors and patterns. I preferred
them, even if Andy didn't understand that.

There's *one* game I almost always win: Memory.

The others are also quite good at it. It's fun when we play together.

When I wanted to show Tina my tricks, like how to better keep track of the cards, she became furious.

"Show-off!" she hollered. "I want to figure it out myself."

When I don't have enough confidence in myself to go down the giant slide alone, I ask Benjamin if he wants to slide down with me. We're very close friends. With him, I'm not scared at all.

My Mom often says: "You did well!"
When I'm unsure of myself, she sometimes asks:
"Do *you* believe you can do it?"
And, suddenly, I become very brave.

I like when Dad asks me:
"What would *you* like to do?"

He often says, "Yes! You can do it!"

My friend always says: "Let's try again!"
if something doesn't work out.
This makes me feel better.

I am brave enough to tell adults if something is not okay by
saying things like: "I won't do that!" or "I don't want that!"
Then I tell them why I don't want to.

If someone is ignoring me, I can get pretty angry.
If I have to, I say loudly: "Listen to me!"

Sometimes adults do things that I don't understand.
I need lots of courage to ask them about it.

Markus once whispered to me,
"You'll be sorry if you tell,"
and I knew that something wasn't right.
It's not tattling if you're revealing bad secrets
that can hurt someone.

About the Author & Illustrator

Holde Kreul was born in 1944 in Szczecin. She studied psychology and focused above all on children with issues. For a long time, she ran a daycare center for children with psychiatric disorders. Now she has her own psychotherapy practice and works with children and adults.

Dagmar Geisler studied drawing in Wiesbaden. Immediately after finishing her degree, she began illustrating books for different publishers. She does this still today with great enthusiasm; she especially likes to come up with funny details for the pictures. Dagmar Geisler has a son and lives with her family near Munich.